MUSEUM OF THE JEWELLERY QTR

MUSEUM OF THE JEWELLERY QUARTER

Birmingham Museums

Front and back cover:
Waist Clasp, 1902-3 designed by Oliver
Baker for WH Haseler & Co

Right: Some of over 7000 metal dies in
the Smith & Pepper workshop

Birmingham Museums

CONTENTS

Claret Jug, 1861-2
by John Hardman & Co (detail)

What is special about Birmingham's Jewellery Quarter?

Today visitors from around the country flock to Birmingham's Jewellery Quarter in their thousands. People have lived and worked in the Quarter since it came into existence, but in recent years they come to shop, to visit a growing number of excellent museums and places of interest and to enjoy the unique historic feel of the place. Increasingly they come to eat and drink in the well-appointed bars and restaurants, whose existence can be attributed in part to a growing community of young professionals who occupy the shiny new flats and houses springing up in the area. The Jewellery Quarter has always been a place of intense human activity.

The Jewellery Quarter is also a place of unique character. The sheer density of one particular trade concentrated in a specific geographical area of a city and the fact that many buildings in the Quarter have been in continual use as jeweller's workshops and residencies since they were built 200 years ago contributes to a sense of stepping back in time. The area is home to the Birmingham Assay Office, which is the busiest site for testing and hallmarking precious metals in the country. And the Quarter is still today the area producing the largest quantity of British made jewellery, a worthy vestige of it having been the one-time largest centre of such production in the world. No wonder so many contemporary designers coming out of the area's world-renowned School of Jewellery set up shop right here in the place where they train and continue to produce fine jewellery alongside firms of long standing.

The Chamberlain Clock

WORTH £1

Birmingham sprang up from very modest beginnings, famously being valued at just £1 in the Domesday Book in 1086. However, certainly by the 14th Century, local smiths were busy making useful metal implements, such as scythes and other cutting tools which they sold to the farmers who crowded into Birmingham on market days. The metalworking industry grew rapidly, overtaking the town's traditional woollen and leather trades. By the 16th century Digbeth and Deritend resounded with the noise of hammers on anvils, according to early visitors who reported that, *'A great parte of the towne is mayntayned by smithes'*. Wealthy landowners coming to town began asking for more ornamental metal goods for their wives and households, and the earliest record of a goldsmith was one John Blakwyn, who we know was working in Birmingham in 1460. But he was unlikely to have been the first!

In 1308 '11 Birmingham pieces' were included on a Knights Templars inventory of personal effects. From their value these are almost certain to have been of precious metals. In 1524 Lord Middleton of Tamworth paid *'the goldesmithe of Byrmyngham'* for making *'IX sponnys (nine spoons) at Dygbethe shoppe'*, and in 1584 the marriage is recorded of Roger Pemberton, goldsmith, who became a leading Birmingham citizen.

Engraving of a goldsmith's workshop in Augsburg, Bavaria by Etienne Delaune, c1576, showing many of the same tools that have been used in Birmingham's Jewellery Quarter over the last 200 years.

"Brummagem Toys"

The origin of jewellery making as a major industry in the town may be said to date from 1660, when King Charles II returned from exile in France after the Civil War. The King brought with him from France a taste for fancy buttons and shoe buckles, considered *'the height of sophisticated fashion'*, starting a fashion here which spread rapidly. He was known to have remarked that Birmingham manufacturers were equal to copying such items and indeed Birmingham metal workers were keen to cater for this new demand. In this way precious metal working grew out of the 'toy' trades – not children's playthings but buckles, buttons, silver and gilt boxes and other small metal trinkets and fashionable personal accessories. 'Brummagem toys' were produced in their hundreds and thousands, in cut steel, silver and gold gaining for the town, by the second half of the 18th century, the accolade, 'the toyshop of Europe'. Contemporary accounts reporting that, *'no other town perhaps in all Europe can equal it...so prevalent is the spirit of industry, so early learnt their children, and practised in riper years, that you won't see an idle person lurking around the streets'.*

Pearl and metal buttons made in Birmingham between 1780 and 1820.

Moving In

Goldsmiths, silversmiths and toymakers were originally scattered across Birmingham, but began to congregate in the Hockley area from the mid-18th century, creating the foundation of what would become known variously as the 'jewellery district', the 'jewellers' quarter', and finally the Jewellery Quarter. The main reason for this was the development of the Colmore family's Newhall estate which released much needed land for housing and manufacture. The craftsmen who set up workshops and lived in this area specialised in particular skills, such as mounters, setters, enamellers and watchmakers. As a group they provided a rich repository of skills which manufacturers could draw upon to meet their orders.

It was both convenient and prudent for the manufacturers to be near to one another. Supporting trades such as tool makers and bullion dealers were also attracted into this area to supply the needs of the trade and so a precious metal working colony settled and became cemented here. The early development of the Jewellery Quarter was largely in the areas of St Paul's Square, Caroline Street, Warstone Lane, Frederick Street, Graham Street and Vittoria Street. St Paul's Church and Square and the neighbouring streets were built in the late 1770s and many of the people who moved into the new houses were prosperous toymakers , silversmiths and goldsmiths and their workers. Workshops were built behind the large houses, while many independent craftsmen worked in a room at home.

Sign of the King's Head, New Street, where Birmingham's first Assay Office opened in 1773

By this time silversmithing had become a major industry in the town. Chief among the silversmiths and toymakers was one of the driving forces of the industrial revolution, the creator of the Soho Manufactory, Lunar Man, steam pioneer, grandfather of modern coinage and all round local celebrity – Matthew Boulton. He led a successful campaign to establish an assay office in Birmingham, with the first assay office opening its doors in a rented room above the King's Head Inn in New Street in 1773, a feat that facilitated the expansion of precious metal working in the town. The assay mark for Birmingham is the anchor.

This may be the result of planning meetings which took place between Matthew Boulton and his Sheffield counterpart in a London public house called The Crown and Anchor. When their petition to parliament for the establishment of two new assay offices was successful, they are reputed to have tossed a coin to see which place would get which symbol, and landlocked Birmingham got the anchor!

Testing and hallmarking are done at an Assay Office, and the Birmingham Assay Office is one of only four in Britain with the others located in London, Sheffield and Edinburgh. Hallmarking began in London in 1300 and is often described as the oldest form of consumer protection in the world.

'Mr Boulton's Manufactory at Soho near Birmingham', c1795-1809 (detail)

The Hallmark

Gold and silver are too soft in their pure form to be used
in jewellery manufacture and have to be alloyed, or mixed
with other metals, to give them extra strength
and hardness.

The proportion of gold to other metals in an alloy is
measured by the CARAT system. Pure gold is said to
be 24 carat. There are four legally acceptable gold alloy
standards in Britain: 22 carat, 18 carat, 14 carat and
9 carat.

An alloy may not look any different from the pure metal,
so gold, silver and platinum jewellery above a certain
weight must be tested to check that the metal meets the
legally acceptable standard, and hallmarked to show that
this has been done. A full hallmark also shows who made
the item, where it was marked, and when.

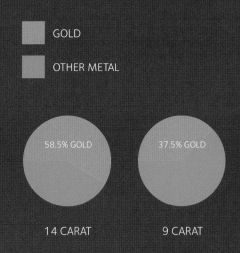

GOLD

OTHER METAL

100% GOLD   91.6% GOLD   75% GOLD   58.5% GOLD   37.5% GOLD

24 CARAT   22 CARAT   18 CARAT   14 CARAT   9 CARAT

CITY OF A THOUSAND TRADES

The jewellery trade has always been vulnerable to changing fashions, as is apparent from the decline of the buckle making trade in the early 1800s, a result of the growing popularity for shoe-strings that were previously considered to be 'unmanly.' The buckle-makers diversified and redeployed their skills into the jewellery trade, as did the button makers in the 1820s when the fashion for large gilt buttons started to decline in preference for smaller pearl and glass buttons. So, from being a specialist branch of the Brummagem toy trade the jewellery trade became established as a trade in its own right in the town in the 1820s.

The development of the canal network in the 18th century contributed greatly to the development of industry in Birmingham. Reaching the town in 1769 it connected Birmingham with the coal mines of the Black Country and therefore facilitated the transport of raw materials as well as finished goods and by 1772 the Newhall terminus was completed in the southern part of the Quarter.

The coming of the railways in the 19th century had the same impact as the earlier canals as well as encouraging the movement of people, enabling more people to migrate and settle in the *'City of a Thousand Trades'*.

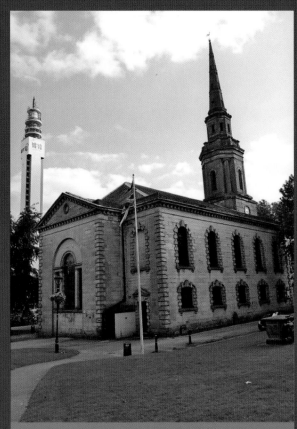

St. Pauls Church, consecrated 1779

In 1848 Vyse Street, Pitsford Street and Hylton Street were built and Branston Street and Spencer Street were extended. This was during a period of unparalleled growth in the size and fortunes of the Birmingham jewellery trade which occurred between 1847 and 1857. The great mid-19th century gold rushes in California and Australia meant that more gold was available than ever before with a greater demand for jewellery from a growing and wealthier population. This demand was met with the introduction of mass production methods and a new, lower 9 carat gold standard which was introduced in 1854. Before this jewellers' were legally obliged to work in the more expensive 18 or 22 carat gold. At only 37.5% pure gold, 9 carat gold was much more affordable to the middle classes, further fueling the booming industry.

The initial population of Vyse Street, the street occupied by the Museum of the Jewellery Quarter, counted 21 jewellers and a diverse collection of inhabitants including school mistresses, surgeons and music professors alongside manufacturers of pistols, pocket books, hooks and eyes and ribbons. Other Trades were gradually ousted as the century progressed by the growing number of jewellers and silversmiths colonising the Quarter's houses. It was written that, *'Kings ransoms could hardly buy the contents of these little, old fashioned, unpretentious houses, where from great safes hidden away in corners, there could be produced for the inspection of the duly accredited enquirer examples of exquisite art, resplendent with gems of purest ray serene!'*.

Detail of J Piggot-Smith's map of Birmingham 1828, showing an increasing number of houses and factories built over fields and gardens as the Quarter took shape.

Self Help

In September 1887 the Birmingham Jewellers' and Silversmiths' Association was formed, and is now a national body, the National Jewellers' Association, still with its headquarters in Birmingham's Jewellery Quarter. The Association's early efforts were mainly concerned with the problems of insolvencies, theft and of foreign competition. They were also keen to address the issue of the poor reputation of Birmingham's goods. London retailers who bought jewellery from Birmingham manufacturers often insisted on having it hallmarked in London so that their wealthy customers would not realise where it was made. The Association tried to improve the reputation of Birmingham made goods by promoting itself through holding an annual dinner with distinguished speakers such as Joseph Chamberlain, and later holding a splendid annual ball showcasing Birmingham-made jewellery.

The Association's main aim was to promote art and technical education amongst apprentice jewellers to raise the general standard of the trade. In 1890, in conjunction with the Municipal School of Art, the Association set up its own school, the Vittoria Street School for Jewellers and Silversmiths. The pupils learned life drawing and modelling as well as the skills of the trade, and the school gained a good reputation. At this time, just men were allowed to train to become jewellers, and only boys were allowed to enrol on the courses. Women were relegated to what were considered 'unskilled' roles, which included polishing and operating fly presses. Today the School of Jewellery continues to thrive with many of the young designer makers and contemporary jewellers learning innovative techniques in jewellery making on the wide range of courses. Women are welcomed, and make up over 70% of current enrolment.

Crowds at Great Hampton street c.1914. One retired worker described how *'on the stroke of one, thousands of men and women emerged from hundreds of workshops, factories and offices and there was then a jostling crowd of humanity stretched across the roads like football crowds...running to catch trams at the bottom of Vyse Street'.*

"WORKSHOP OF THE WORLD"

The jewellery trade was approaching its peak at the beginning of the 20th century and the houses occupied by masters became increasingly converted to workshops as those profiting from the trade moved to leafy suburbs like Edgbaston and Handsworth. The Jewellery Quarter became a jumble of houses, workshops and densely packed courts of back-to-backs to such an extent that it was reported to be the most densely built upon part of Britain. Kathleen Dayus who lived and worked in the Quarter describes it in 1913 as being *so crammed with humanity that it was more like a rabbit's warren.* She grew up in Camden Street in one of the many back-to-back houses in which people working in the trade often lived. They were small, dark houses built round a court with shared privies and washhouses. Another resident of a back-to-back house, Rose born in 1911, describes how *A lot of women used to go and get the safety pins and buttons and card them for a penny and twopence. They used to be have to do a gross, sit up all hours. There was no end of small jewellery places round there then where you could get a job...but the houses were bug ridden, didn't matter how clean you were, you couldn't rest, so during the warm weather we used to sit out on the pavement til about 10 o'clock.*

The Jewellery Quarter was a very close-knit community where everyone knew each other. Many of the young boys who would go on to become apprentices and eventually highly-skilled jewellers started out as errand boys. The Jewellery Quarter abounded with young errand boys, carrying parcels or pushing them in open, three-wheeled baskets. They collected bullion and took goods from workshop to workshop, or to the Assay Office for hallmarking. Sometimes boys would leave their baskets or put down their bags while they had a game of marbles or football, using the parcels of gold as goal posts!

Recruiting poster, 5th Battalion Royal
Warwickshire Regiment, Jewellers'
Companies, c1914
*'Young men who join have the satisfaction
of knowing that they are training
themselves to be fit for the defence of their
country at the time of need.'*

There was a repeat of this process during the Second World War, when once again war work occupied those who stayed at home. In 1942 there was a ban on the manufacture of jewellery, except items that were seen as essential such as clocks, watches and cufflinks. Wedding rings had traditionally been made in 22ct gold, but during the war only utility wedding rings were made and these were of 9ct gold. Recovery after the war was very difficult with problems such as manpower shortage, insufficient materials and the pressure to win back the export markets.

Sylvia Darbey, later wife of David Wright of the company Wright & Hadgkiss describes the Jewellery Quarter in the post-war years *'...it was a very close-knit community, with two or three firms sharing an old house as their premises. Everyone knew everyone else (and often their business too) and a state of friendly rivalry*

**TERRITORIAL ARMY
FORCES BILL.**

**Proposed Raising of
Two Companies of Jewellers
and Silversmiths.**

A PUBLIC

MEETING

WILL BE HELD AT

**ST. PAUL'S SCHOOLS, SPENCER STREET,
BIRMINGHAM,**

ON

MONDAY NEXT, THE 17TH FEBRUARY

AT 7 P.M.

**ALL MEN between the ages of 18 & 35
INVITED to ATTEND.**

W. G. MOORE & CO., PRINTERS, SCOTLAND PASSAGE, HIGH STREET, BIRMINGHAM.

existed throughout. It was impossible to step outside without meeting old friends or acquaintances...Old jewellers never retired – they faded away. Scores continued working long after retirement age. In many family firms the owners still clocked in every day, sometimes into their 80s and 90s'.

It is believed that the firm TL Mott, which occupied premises now housing parts of the Museum, made miniature compasses concealed in rings during the Second World War, to help captured POWs to escape and make their way back home, a history which has always been shrouded in secrecy. Motts were founded in 1875 establishing a show room and workshop at 79 Vyse Street and then extending into no 80 in 1926. They traded until 1972, and were famous for making butterfly wing jewellery, using the colourful wings of exotic butterflies to create pictures on powder boxes and cigarette cases as well as jewellery.

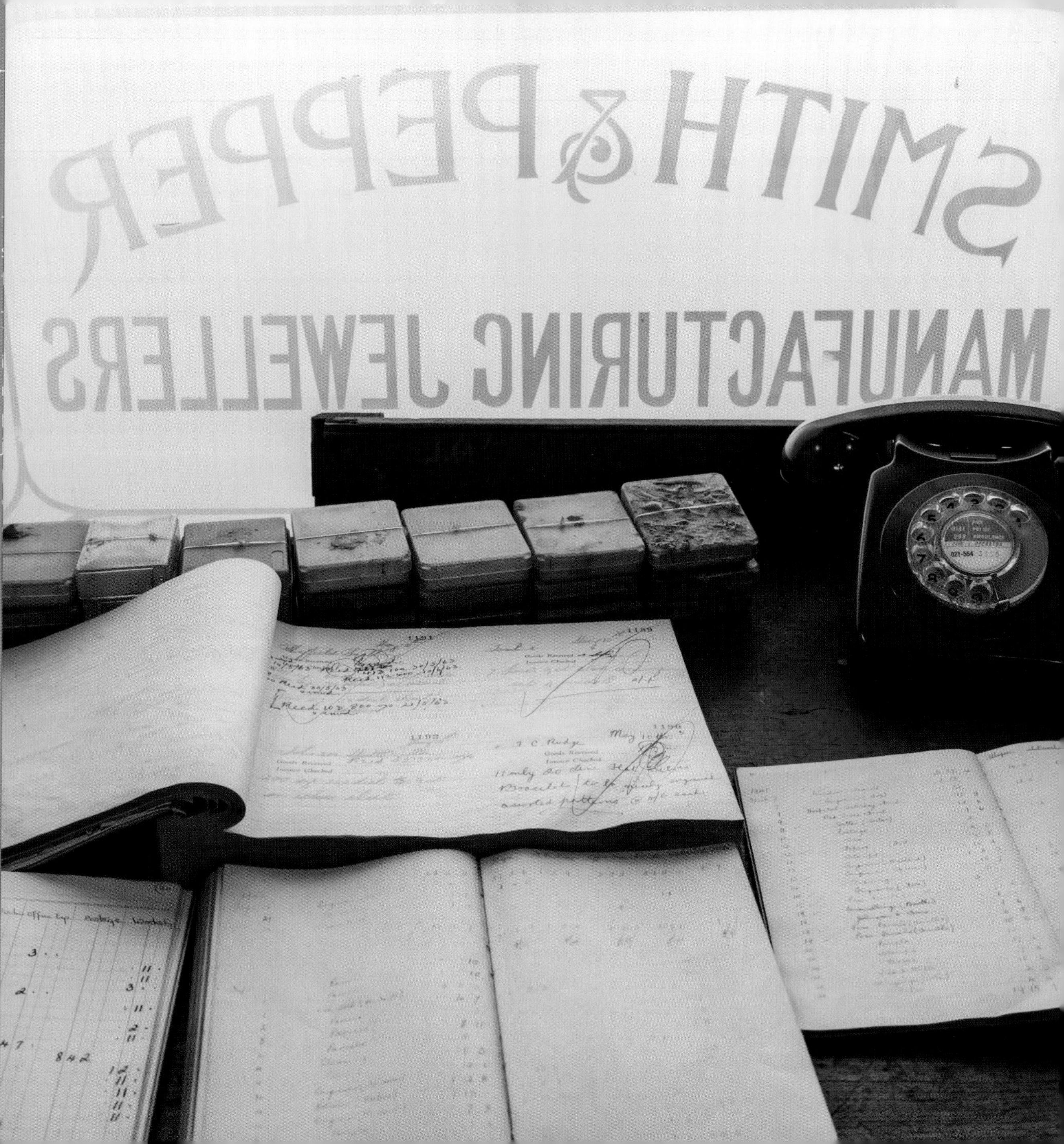
SMITH & PEPPER
MANUFACTURING JEWELLERS

Smith & Pepper: A Family Firm

The Museum of the Jewellery Quarter is built around the historic workshops of an old family-run Jewellery Quarter company, Smith & Pepper.

The founders were Charles Smith (1867-1933) and Edwin Pepper (1858-1935). Edwin Pepper was Charles Smith's uncle and they both worked in Charles Smith's father's jewellery manufacturing firm, Smith & Ewen. In 1899 Charles Smith and Edwin Pepper left Smith & Ewen to go into partnership as Smith & Pepper, registering their mark at Birmingham Assay Office on 5 September 1899.

The company's address was 77/78 Vyse Street, which was then two terraced houses rented from the owner, Frank Moore, who was married to Charles Smith's sister Jane. Charles Smith and his wife lived at no.77 for a time, where the first of their nine children, Charles Eric (always known as Eric) was born in 1900. The single storey workshop at the back was built around the time the business started, over the former garden.

From the start, Smith & Pepper made gold bangles, brooches, cufflinks, lockets and crosses, and continued making many of the same designs throughout their history, specialising in bracelets. They were particularly well known for 'snake' armlets and necklets, and for 'bamboo' bangles and therefore it is no surprise that their telegraphic address was 'ARMLET, BIRMINGHAM'.

Charles Smith

Edwin Pepper

By 1914 the business was doing well enough to replace the two old houses with a new front office block, linked to the old workshop at the back. The architect was a family relation, G.E.Pepper.

During the 1920s Charles Smith's son Eric and daughter Olive joined the business. Their father retired in the early 1930s and another son, Thomas, came into the firm.

When Charles Smith died in 1933, Eric and Tom became the new partners, with Olive as company secretary. The three siblings continued to run the business in a virtually unchanged fashion until 1981, when they decided they had had enough, and the company ceased trading. Eric was then 81, Olive 78 and Tom 74 and there were no direct heirs to take over the business.

Passage

The short passage leading from the first floor displays into the Smith & Pepper offices has photographs of the founders of the company, Charles Smith and his uncle Edwin Pepper, together with Charles' nine sons and daughters and some of their employees. The case shows examples of the firm's jewellery and papers.

1

2

Mr Eric's Office

In the small private office special customers were received, watched over by the portrait of Winston Churchill.

Miss Olive's Office

In the main office orders were recorded and passed on to the ground floor workshop via the hand-operated lift. Finished jewellery came back up to the office by the same route for invoicing, packing and despatch to customers all over the world. Tea and toast were served daily in the office, with Marmite or home-made jam. 'Upstairs' and 'dowsnstairs' staff rarely mixed. The office and its contents are as they were left in 1981.

1. Smith & Pepper trade catalogue, c1914
2. Jewellery made by Smith & Pepper
3. Offices at Smith & Pepper
4. Cardboard boxes ready for despatch

WORKSHOPS

WORKSHOPS

Weighing Gold: Each morning Tom Smith ('Mr Tom') weighed the gold in the front room on the ground floor and issued it to the craftsmen, noting the amount in the ledger. At night, finished and unused metal were weighed back in and again recorded.

Machines: Around the workshop are various machines from different periods of the company's history. They include powered wire drawing machines, rollers, and an engine turning machine. Although Smith & Pepper was a very traditional company, it did invest in a diamond milling machine, which produced bright facets on gold. This was installed in the 1960s and is the most modern machine in the workshop, and the first of its kind in the Quarter.

Dies: There are around 7,000 steel dies on the wall racks that were used to stamp and cut out the gold or silver components for the jewellery. The components were first formed using the heavy drop stamps at the far end of the workshop, operated by a man (one man, Arthur Brewer, worked on these drop stamps from 1920–1981). They were then cut out on the smaller fly presses, which were operated by women.

Benches: Craftsmen worked close together, several to a bench, assembling the stamped parts, soldering, filing and engraving. There were up to 37 people working in the factory during its busiest period, making it a moderately large company.

The traditional jeweller's bench is cut out to allow the jewellers to sit close to the work, and is fairly high so that the work is at a comfortable height without having to bend over it. Many of the hand tools still used in the trade have hardly changed for centuries and can easily be recognised on old drawings of workshops.

Cellar: The cellar is not open to visitors but large bags in the cellar can be seen through the viewing panel in the floor by the main bench. These were part of a suction system which collected dust from the long

bank of polishing and lapping machines, and water from hand-washing were all saved and filtered to extract the gold dust, which was melted down in a small furnace in the cellar, along with the scrap. This melted scrap and gold dust was either added to new gold or sold to a refiners, and the firm produced its own alloys, mainly 9 and 18 carat.

Finishing: At the polishing machines along one wall of the workshop women and girls polished the jewellery which was a dirty job. Violet, who worked as a polisher at Smith and Pepper in the 1920s recalls that *'It was noisy- spindles were belt driven; there was a box at the back to catch the polishings. Later they had an extraction system. Our faces used to get dirty. We used to fix a big sheet of brown paper all down our fronts to catch the dust but our faces got filthy. We used polishing rouge and a long stick of brown stuff to polish. There were racks (metal foot scrapers) on the floor, they took the dust off your feet, they were swept up each week'.*

BACK TO LIFE

When Smith & Pepper closed down in 1981 papers were left scattered in the office, and downstairs in the workshop, tools, tea mugs and cigarette packets were left strewn on the benches. For many years they remained undisturbed.

When work began in 1990 the first task was to empty the Smith & Pepper building. The Ironbridge Institute photographed and catalogued everything where it lay, before removing some 70,000 items for safekeeping - from the milk bill for 1899, found in the attic, to the machines on the ground floor.

Derelict no.79 next door which had been the jewellery workshop of another firm, T L Mott was rebuilt to provide modern visitor facilities and display space, and then in 2009 the museum was developed through the expansion into no 80 which provided more gallery space, and a tea room.

The Smith & Pepper building also needed to be repaired and restored. Wiring had to be brought up to date and there was a long search for old-fashioned style three-core maroon flex which would meet present standards without looking out of place. It was finally supplied by a manufacturer specialising in period electrical props for films.

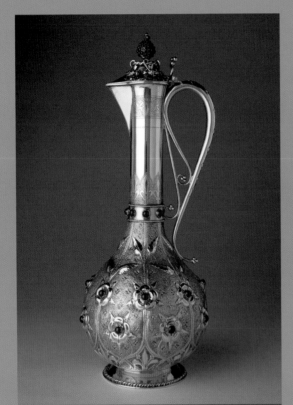

Claret Jug, 1861-2 by John Hardman & Co, Hardmans were based in the Jewellery Quarter

Everything was then put back in its place, right down to the ageing jars of Marmite and home-made jam in the office and the overalls hanging up in the factory.

Former Smith & Pepper employees who came back to see the result gave it their seal of approval: *'Yes, this is how it was; this is just how it was.'*

Since opening to the public in 1992, the Museum of the Jewellery Quarter has gone from strength to strength. It is the recipient of several prestigious awards, including winning Best Small Visitor Attraction in Visit England's Awards for Excellence in 2010, and it regularly tops the charts on TripAdvisor. Judges and visitors wax lyrical about the enthusiastic and knowledgeable staff, the sense of stepping back in time and the feeling of having discovered a time capsule, a glimpse of working life that could so easily have been lost. Long-established businesses in the Quarter have come to see it as their museum, telling stories about their work and lives, and are quick to offer objects and archives on loan for exhibitions.

Brown Bakelite fittings were no longer available, so new brass ones were powder coated in brown to resemble them. Broken windows were replaced with new ones, etched to match the originals and paint colours were carefully matched.

The museum continues to support local designer makers by exhibiting their work and selling it in the shop, and by employing them to give fascinating workshops for children and adults. Whatever your reason for visiting – you are sure to feel truly immersed in the proud heritage of this unique area of the City of Birmingham.

Bibliography & Further Reading

J. Catell, B. Hawkins, *The Birmingham Jewellery Quarter: An Introduction and guide* (2015)

J. Catell, *The Birmingham Jewellery Quarter: An Architectural Survey of the Manufactories.* (2002)

K. Dayus, *The Girl From Hockley.* (2006)

J. Debney, *Jewels of Our City: Birmingham's Jewellery Quarter.* (2013)

S. Mason, *Jewellery Making in Birmingham.* (1998)

Acknowledgements

This guide was edited by Oliver Buckley, Rachel West, Laura Cox and Barbara Nomikos with support from Rupert Fisher and the rest of the team at the Museum of Jewellery Quarter.

This guidebook is based on original research and texts by Shena Mason (1938-2014) and is dedicated to her memory.

Photography of the Smith & Pepper Factory by David Rowan.

Picture Credits

Page 8   A goldsmith's workshop
           (first engraving), Delaune, Etienne
           (1519-1583), c1576
           ©The Trustees of the British Museum.
           All rights reserved

Page 10   Kings Head
           ©Birmingham Assay Office

Page 20   Women working at the Deakin
           and Francis factory
           ©Deakin and Francis

All other images copyright Birmingham Museums.